POETIC
of a
CAMERON HIGHLANDER

POETIC JOURNAL
—————— *of a* ——————
CAMERON HIGHLANDER

Poems written by a soldier
during the 2nd World War

Jack Gillespie

HISTORY INTO PRINT

First published by
History into Print, 56 Alcester Road,
Studley, Warwickshire B80 7LG in 2009
www.history-into-print.com

ISBN: 978-1-85858-329-7

A Cataloguing in Publication Record
for this title is available from the British Library

Typeset in Book Antiqua
Printed in Great Britain by
Cpod, Trowbridge, Wiltshire

CONTENTS

OBSERVATIONS & COMMENTS

This book is the property of Pte. Gillespie J.
(ex 2927948) *now* <u>Mr John Gillespie</u> *Bart!*
7 Platoon, 'A' Coy.

2nd Bn. QUEEN'S OWN CAMERON HLDRS

This book is written at various intervals in my Army career, its primary object is to enable the youngsters Ron, Don, Malcolm and any "curious" individual, to get a glimpse of a soldier's thoughts and deeds, or mis-deeds. It being written during my sojourn in the services, I cannot stress enough the futility, misery, complete hopeless-ness of War. Comradeship is the only good that emerges, and one can only hope that it will remain, when the present War is finished. Your Uncle Bill seldom told of his experiences in World War 1914-18, but when he did, he mentioned piling up the dead, bloated, smelly, and then digging holes to bury them. Stan and I heard but apparently took not enough heed, we fancied the Sunday Church Parade with a Pipe Band, the 14 days in the Isle of Man. When war was imminent and the R.A were called up, the fact that The Liverpool Scottish were not mobilised was a sore point with us. We wanted to hear the guns, to do a bit of hand-to-hand fighting, after being first half paralysed by a frenzied crowd of mob-worshippers.

The matter of 10 years will see you all lined up, in a similar frame of mind, I feel sure that, as sure as Friday follows Thursday, youth knows it all, he wants a sample of everything. Now this is the sample of all samples, you get thrills, and it is the very counterpart of the school game Chase –me Charlie. It's not a boy with a belt that goes after you, it's bits of lead and old scrap iron, no scarcity, bags of it, far more than a piece each. Just to make things more exciting you have to put your feet down kind of "canny", or else you go up like a Roman Candle. You have to find some fine hiding places, for they send planes to look for you. Human Nature is a queer thing, remember how you wanted some hand-to-hand fighting, now is your chance, but knowing the scene is set, you don't fancy it, in fact it's the one thing you do not want, you want to be a million miles away, and it's touch and go whether you can stand it. You want the earth to swallow you up and maybe, your mind is thinking in terms of how a Tommy Gun could go off. You remember not how you relied on that hand for the scrapping at the club. That thought passes, and you just keep on thinking of picture queues, and beer houses, and how you would not join a Christmas Club if given the chance. You have a pal haven't you, well, I had too, but he was 23, fancied Navy clothes, but Arthur Griffiths was drowned early on.

Now lads this isn't written to frighten you, I am going to say I hope you grow up, to have all it takes, but with a headpiece that can absorb some straight talk and deep thinking. Let your generation put as much into

1

winning a peace as the last two have into K.O'ing Germany's military efforts. If you ever fancy War read "All Quiet on the Western Front" author Erich M. Remarque.

That's all except there are no cheering crowds, the only send off you get 'three raspberries and this ship's hooter'.

J. Gillespie.

SATURDAY – THE INVASION OF SICILY
(Written at 4pm ## July 1943).

Today being Saturday, but that day being nothing but the day that follows Friday, I being in pensive mood desire to set down in writing, the passing thoughts of a most, useless soldier. Since having had the news of Stan's commission, followed by his becoming a Paratroop, I must confess to clear my own conscience, the reasons for my static position. I am under no illusions as to my safe passage so far, that is good fortune and as I see it the luck of the draw. My chances of becoming a Paratroop have sunk to zero, as the C.O. will not release us from this unit. Still the vision of a dead man wrapped in a blanket (for which payment will have to be made out of his credits) take the shine out of glorious deeds. Likewise the sight of men without any legs, do not increase the urge. In passing I must pay tribute to these wounded Guardsmen, Infanteers, Signallers, Artillerymen and Engineers as they go down to hospital. One Glasgow boy with both legs off is singing "I belong to Glasgow". (Hells Bells). The cigarette is such help to them all, that it makes me ponder as to what outlet my nerves will have, should anything happen to me.

I hear the Hampshires have caught a packet, what an unlucky crew. (Late News).

J. Gillespie.

FAVOURITE LINES

Sentimental.

1. They grow not old – as we that are left grow old,
   Age shall not weary them, or the years condemn,
   At the going down of the sun
   And in the morning,
   We will remember them.

   (Laurence Binyon).

   ---

2. The beauty of this house is order,
   The blessing of the house is contentment,
   The glory of the house is hospitality.

   (House Motto).

   ---

3. Lead Kindly Light, amid the encircling gloom,
   Lead thou me on,
   The night is dark, and I am far from home,
   Lead thou me on,
   Keep thou my feet, I do not ask to see,
   The distant scene,
   One step enough for me.

4. Mad-dogs and Englishmen go out in the Mid-day sun. (Quotation)

5. A Cynic – A blackguard who sees things as they really are, and not as they ought to be. (Ambrose Bierce)

5a. Cowards die many times before their death. (Julius Ceasar)

6. It's good to have money, and the things money can buy, but it's good too, to check up once in a while, and make sure you haven't lost the things money can't buy. (Geo. Horace Lorimer).

7. I do not regret this journey, which has shown that Englishman can endure hardship, help one another, and meet death with as great a fortitude as ever in the past. We took risks, we had to, there must be an element of risk, we bow to the Will of Providence, determined to do our best to the last.

   (Scott's last expedition).

OUR CANTEEN *(11 verses)*

Aloof it stands from all the rest
Of all the tents, it is the best.
A soldiers poem of delight,
At least upon a Thursday night.

Just take a peep inside it, Sir,
You'll see the business manager,
He went to school with Harry Lauder,
You'll appreciate that – when he takes your order.

Your in no hurry, it doesn't matter,
Just stand and listen to his patter,
You've stacks of time – as through notes he wades,
To see if you owe him for 2 'Pal' Blades.

What's this here, is it trouble brewing,
He'd boot polish last year – and should know there's nothing doing.
The manager has squared things with a ready smile,
And explained if he's good he will get one in a while.

Eighty fags – nearly 12 per day,
There are no sweets, but one P.K.
"You want your beer then" O.K. Jock,
These canteen chitties are all to cock.

We're not like H.Q., with tobacco,
I'll tell you what you can have a badge though,
Or what about a Khaki Hanky,
says the salesman from Killiecrankie.

When through the week, the cry's Buckshees,
all his cronies he'll try to please,
His own ration, he sells to Six,
Its amazing where, he learnt his tricks.

When you're at the counter, full of hope,
You hear your washings off – it's not your turn for Soap,
Maybe you turn away, and shed a little tear,
But its abandon all hope, ye that enter here.

This man must remain Anonymous,
With his motto "One for me and none for us",
He's got more cash than Rank or Korda,
And he's got it stacked – just over the Border.

He knows four names in history though,
They're not Longstop or Anzio,
They're the days he drew a pay you see,
To show he was still in the Company.

He's not a bad chap – so we say,
I hear the lads say so each day,
Say shall I spell his name out yet,
By Hell – I will, it is BURNET.

CLOSETs NOT ALL WCs

MacLean – *Kicking a dying 'Jerry' up a hill*

Walker – *Just filthy.*

Lt. Dowson – *Afraid to acknowledge me until we met on an invasion craft. – Must tell Stan.*

Sgt. Burns – *Africa Star rampant – How the devil did he get made up.*

Major Duff – *Upon my departure for the front " I wish you luck, and hope you'll come through" (He had spent weeks trying to get me there).*

Jack Gettings – *A Bridgend Scrum-half, a terrific tackler and yet panic stricken of getting shot. (Which he did).*

Bob Seaward – *Killed himself when on guard – with a fit of the blues.*

THE TWO TYPES *(7 verses)*

No, not the men from the 8ths own news,
Or ones with different political views,
But the ones who dig the deepest hole,
In which we "turf" our inner soul.

The Grammar School Boy has hair of red,
And a boozing life he always led.
While the graduate from Drunkin & Mawdlyn
Professor Goodwin I mean is never Dawdlin.

They're always happy at their work,
Clean all seats, – They never shirk,
And smells that nearly turn us sick though,
To them is just like Good Old Bisto.

In olden days the common soldier,
Emptied the buckets, as sergeants told yer,
But now we have these landed gentry,
Sprinkling Chloride ere our entry.

They make the place so cute & neat,
With different size & shape of seat,
It always makes you realize one thing
For once you're really doing something.

It's a treat to hear their Oxford twang,
Instead of awful Townee slang,
And to hear them not say hey' here you,
But Pardon me dear Montague.

Epilogue

Such Pioneers in our history – we cannot let pass,
These men who put Sanitary in Upper Class,
So they'll wear cross closets & Toilet Roll,
Until they return to "Live on the Dole".

SENTIMENT:

I was in Scotland most of my service in Blighty, and I well remember at Killwhinning we were billeted in Nissen Huts. One of the boys had his wife killed in a blitz on Manchester, leaving him with two children. As far as the Army went, he did not belong to it, he scarce ever paraded, and just stared at the N.C.O.s when they 'bawled' him out. His name was Lockett and he was a solo cornet player in one of these Championship Brass Bands. It was often an occurrence his playing about 10 o'clock at night, 'Somewhere a voice is calling', to the photograph of his wife, that he had on a shelf over his bed. The way those notes used to pierce through the night shadows was something terrifying, one could sense that his wife was a very "present" listener to his serenade.

PRESENTIMENT:

We sat outside a gun pit, and Bryn Rees was laying the law down that he would prove a better man that I when the time came, however, the trouble was mostly due to his being a "detailed" volunteer to go with us. It was as well no money was on it, with foot blown off, he neither cried or passed out for quite a while, and one must be forced to the conclusion that he knew how he was going to take it.

PREDICAMENT:

In St. Ruprecht we found a young Hungarian girl about 16, she had a baby on order, it wouldn't be long before the van called. It was an English soldier that took the order, a devout lover he "Baled" out near the zero hour. In his conceited manner he had left a highly expensive, large framed photograph of himself playing at his famous Cinema Organ.

WAR COMMENTARY *(by a spy)*

1.   Due to some pressure from the Govt. men wholly employed on Essential Work, were also forced to register for essential C.D. duty. Uncle Jack S., found himself after due deliberation presenting his credentials for enrolment in the Home Guard. "Well" said a public spirited chunk of dynamite at the counter, "You've taken long enough to come", "In that case" said Uncle Jack, "if you feel that way about it, keep it".

   (The new discipline we all dreamt about).

2.   The Air Raid Shelter 2. Bellairs Rd.,
   May almost fell in as the last wails of the siren faded away, with an armful of Gas masks, Blankets & books. On the kit check, Ma Gates found her mask missing. "That's right" she said: "just look after yourselves, never mind me", "there is almost certain to be Gas dropped tonight"
   No one got out though – Pop was going to chance it but was stopped.

GILLESPIE'S REGIMENTALLY EMPLOYED

(from Nov. 20th 1945 till ......)

You've no doubt heard of Mr Wu,
And all the washing he did do,
But now the Queens Own do present,
An Establishment whose aim is bent,
On Washing Whiter than the snow,
Clothes for men on Sentry go.

Of course the other 90% per cent.
Have their dirty bundles sent
And to show they have no favourites,
The same attention one & all gets.
Be it Vests or Khaki shirt,
Soiled with oil or just plain dirt.

It boasts no names like New or Model,
Or adverts saying works a doddle,
Nor guarantees to Iron & Press,
In half an hour or even less,
But it stands there so symbolic
This house of Lifebouy & Carbolic.

The Staff is mainly feminine,
Age from 40 to 59,
They are Virgins one & all,
Fat, tall, thin and small,
Fondling with Angelic Hands,
The clothes we've brought from other lands.

Presiding over all & sundry,
From Mondays morn till even Sunday,
Is a dodging duty Lance Naik,
Call him, what you will or like,
His the power to pull the strings
Of Pyjama Trousers & other things.

For once he really is Tee-chai,
Gosh! Promotion, Riding High,
He orders up his female slaves,
To soap the suds & part the waves,
Orders one to bring his tea,
While another sweeps the Lavatory.

I doubt if medals he will get,
For drying washing that was wet,
But he has the satisfaction
Of seeing his work go into action,
The Persil Whiteness of the boys,
The Inspecting Officer so enjoys.

Order of the day,
Gillespie expects that every man this day will do his duty,
Sending socks for laundrying by an 'Itye' cutie,
Washing all bar sins away,
Doing it for a Soldiers Pay,
While all you do sit back and wait,
As you go out – Just note the plate.

There will now be a pause of two minutes for those that
held these R./E. jobs down during hostilities.
After all anyone can do it now, but it was a good man that
could then.

THE UNFINISHED

It's long ago that I went away,
But longer still since I went to play
At Soldiers, on a Barrack Square,
And listen to the Sergeant Swear.

I thought I knew a thing or two,
They said scrap that – we'll teach it you,
We've got it all down in a book,
To dig, to shoot, to fight, to cook.

We did our drills in numbers then,
The Eighteens and the married men,
We doubled round and did P.T.
Except for those that joined M.T.

Battle Courses – we ran, one after t'other,
Imprecations were hurled that we had no mother,
"Get that head down" Help one another,
Crikey! The dust, I'm sure I will smother.

Then came the day you'd 3 months in,
Seven days home, you'd soon begin,
To see the baby grown so big,
To take the wife a Thing-a-me-jig.

What did you care if the rain did pelter,
Or you sat all night, out in the shelter,
You felt it in your inner soul,
That you were safe down in that hole.

You learnt to drive the measured mile,
According to drill book, Army style,
Left hand down, and such and such,
We're telling you, you'll double declutch.

Then came the very fateful day,
They gave you a pass, and 3 weeks pay,
Yes this was It, it was embarkation,
You walked in a daze, down to the station.

For a day or two, you don't say nowt,
Then comes the day you let it out,
And the wife & you just hug each other,
Keep back the tears, and go to tell mother.

The doorbell rings, you stand forlorn,
A telegram to you is borne,
"Return at once" and makes a mention,
That if you don't it means detention.

You take off your civvies – and bid them farewell,
Parting quite sadly, with your patents as well,
Everyone feels it, the babe & Aunt Nelly,
You have such a sinking inside of your belly.

The finest of dinners before you is placed,
You know you can't eat it – it will go to waste,
Then you grab all your kit – and make for the door,
You hug & you kiss as never before.

Time flies and soon you land at a Port,
No names, Careless Talk, we've been well taught,
The boat is there waiting, we show no elation,
The gangplank is 80 degrees elevation.

You stagger round decks, down an Iron Stair,
You just make a slip, then fly through the Air,
But soon you are jammed – there's no room to fall,
The whole British Army – Tom Cobleigh an all.

You wonder which Army the Eighth or the First,
Whichever it is you're fearing the worst,
It's not that your windy – you'd just like to see,
A few of the wives of Mohammed Imshee.

The first foreign city you see is Algiers,
You're not going there though, no blinking fears,
Get on that "Combined Ops" for a sail down Bomb Alley,
The sirens wail out, you give them a Rally.

The crew all Royal Navy – seem very cool,
Nothing can hit us – don't be a fool
This is quite true – for lo & behold,
We land at the place-without being "holed".

We get off the ship, piled up with gear,
It's not like at home, there's no bands out here,
You realize the reasons, the hurry to clear,
As out of the clouds some "Jerries" appear.

We march off for transit, through the fine sand,
After 3 hours marching, we're scarce able to stand,
At 7 o'clock there's one mile to go,
At 9 it's the same – Oh Hell you all know.

At last we arrive with backs nearly broken,
And to us these kind words are soon being spoken,
"I'm sorry there's no tea or food for tonight,
You're forbidden to smoke or show a light".

You get hold of some Oranges, maybe for nix,
And soon you have put – away about six,
You hope that a closets somewhere near,
Yes you've got the feeling you have Diarrhoea.

Six days of ease, then on your way,
The transport has landed here today,
You're in a truck with Ammunition,
If you get "hit" you're a "cert" for Perdition.

You arrive at Ref. Point, go into action,
Told by the "Brig" you give satisfaction,
"A bloody good show, really quite pukka",
You're wondering if all is OK with your "mucker".

Then comes that glorious day in May,
The Allied might – Von Arnim can't stay,
Tunis is ours – Bizerta too,
Jerry & Ities have had it the noo.

Liverpool Scottish Regiment at camp before the outbreak of War.
Courtesy of 'The Liverpool Scottish Museum Trust'.

My brother Stan is in the centre.

Yours truly is second from the right.

B.L.A. *v.* "D" DAY DODGERS

(Infanteers from each theatre)

We find it pretty hard to say,
Who fought the harder in their day,
The hardest contest
The Greater Conquest
The Middle East or West

Take the miles they went from home,
Through mighty waves and frothy foam,
The longest way,
November not May
The Middle East or West.

They'd each a new "lingo" to speak,
To help when food or dames they seek,
Combien – Gay Paree,
Quanta Costa – Italy,
The Middle East or West.

The Liberators know the Yankee Slang,
While we adopt the Arab twang,
God-dam Baby,
Arouha – Imshee,
The Middle East or West.

One trained in the land of hills & Lochs,
The other in sand and sweaty socks,
Draught Beer,
No water here,
The Middle East or West.

June 6th 44, we made the invasion,
Sicily and Salerno were before that occasion,
Very Risky
Same Tredisky
The Middle East or West.

Yes we fought throughout a year or more,
Oh we'd begun three years before,
Hellish Rhine,
Similar El Alamein
Middle East or West.

Three Yanks to one of us were sent,
The Med was British 75% per cent,
Underground Workers,
Johnny Gurkas,
In Middle East or West.

We cleaned up "V" sites pretty nippy,
We put-in attacks on hills so slippy,
Dainty Mam'as-elle
Dames like Hobs of Hell
The Middle East or West.

We stormed the beaches, hell they ran,
Did that Highland Div. get out to you old man,
One Bagpipe Burst
Oh! the 51st,
The Middle East or West.

Monty led us on the Victory
We'd a difference with him o'er this P.T,
Bernard Law,
Heard it before,
In Middle East or West.

Our petrol stoves were covered in dust,
No troubles there, we'd a Brew Can bust,
Petrol Pipes,
The two types,
Oh! the Middle East or West.

Our Don Rs. got there with the mail,
Ours too were seldom known to fail,
French Letters
Italian Letters
Oh Middle East or West.

This was the War to end all Wars,
Ours was the one, to give us sores,
Vin Blanc,
Multi Stonk,
The Middle East or West.

Realization

I can see we Dodged as well as thee,
And I suppose we Liberated Italy,
Viva Joe,
Hail Amigo,
The Middle East greets West.

Now this is the verse to end all verses,
Written with a thousand curses,
Home next week,
Home NEXT YEAR
Middle East or West.

STOP – READ ON

The date is 5th October, I am on leave, I play with a little girl, her name is Cynthia Heys; she lives in No.5 Banstead Grove. Her age is only 6½ years, she is happy because I find time to play with her. In time she says to me: **"I wish I had a Dad"**, (I'm all washed up).
    NOTE: Her Dad was drowned at sea.

// Write nothing, thoughts can fill pages //

GUARD MOUNTING

Get Marching up & down, !
He shouts and causes us to frown,
And swing the arm that's disengaged,
Before you get me quite enraged.

You chosen men of company guard,
Will find the mounting pretty hard,
So watch your blinking step or I,
Will put you in the cells forebye.

It's names I'm after here tonight,
For extra duties not too light,
Be sure that he that makes a slip,
Will be held firmly in my grip.

Form up means the show is on,
For all the folks to gaze upon,
He calls out for the shining star,
Ben Baxter the Manchester Havildar.

Number One's equipment passes,
Number Two has faulty brasses,
Four is booked for bayonet rusty,
Six for having Rifle dusty.

In case you fancy this Cameron show,
And to the performance would "aye" go,
They mount at Six and then at Seven,
And not as of yore at nine & eleven.

(Curtailed due to loss of Original)

WITH APOLOGIES TO
"WOODBINE WILLIE"

When Jesus came to Birmingham
   They simply passed him by.
They never hurt a hair of him
   They simply let him die.

For men had grown more tender
   And they would not give him pain.
They only just passed down the street
   And left him in the rain.

Still Jesus cried forgive them for
   They know not what they do
And still it rained the wintry rain
   That drenched him through & through.

The crowds went home and left the
   Streets without a soul to see
And Jesus crouched against the
   Wall and cried for Calvary.

———————

Our padre were a solemn bloke
We called him dismal Jim.
It fairly gave you blooming creeps
To sit and hark at him.
When he were on with Judgement Day
About the great white throne
And how each chap would have to stand
And answer on his own
And if he tried to chance his arm
And hide a single sin
There'd be the Angel Gabriel
With books to do him in.

*The next page of the book was ripped out – no doubt
censored by the adjutant.*

TWO SONNETS TO THOSE
THAT WEAR BONNETS

Sonnet 1.

Observe the chests of Cameron men,
With Rainbow coloured strips ye ken,
Of every hue & colour known,
Upon a little bar they've sewn.
The honours there of all degree
most of them are sporting three,
The Premiere one is Italy
for chasing Jerry o'er these hills
While next to it, wears he who wills,
The one for Blighty supping gills,
Or else for being evacuated,
To Islands geographically situated
Away from Jerrys flying Bombs
And a flying start for "If he comes".

Sonnet 2. (Medal Hunters)

Hagan, Fagin, Finnigan & Doyle,
You've finished with Sweat, and blood & toil,
No more you'll burrow in the soil,
With Temperature that's on the boil,
And Privates, Winkin, Blinkin & Nod,
What you suffered – Oh my God!
You're lucky your not beneath the sod,
So slap those medals on your chest,
Across that skinny shepherds pie breast,
On overcoat, pyjamas too,
Ah! Our hands go in salute to you,
You've earned all Civvy Street can give
You've blessing of Sixth Armoured Div.
Sit down you ---s and learn to Live.

Curly Poynter – Handsome Curly started to go off his rocker –
He kept asking Bert Williams and myself not to leave him, he
couldn't be pacified, he made this night Hell for me.

UNDER 26s LAMENT

The joyful day has come at last,
Europe's War is now the past,
And Camerons wait without a murmur,
The call to go and fight in Burma.

The ones whose group is under Twenty,
Can shoot their mouth off good and plenty,
For under the Releasing Plan
They do nix fighting with Japan.

One Volunteer is worth a dozen
I must just tell it to my cousin,
For years he's worked on at munitions
Its his chance to sample our conditions.

He will have to dodge the foul malaria,
Spend lots of time to clean the area,
And for his grub have bowls of Rice
And maybe fishcakes once or twice.

He'll spend much time in jungle fighting
Get balled out for never writing,
He may get hitched up with a Hindoo
And smell more smells than me or you do.

The belts and webbing scrubbed so white
And brasses sparkling oh so bright,
May drop some soldier in the Ack-Ack,
If caught patrolling in the night.

They'll go out girded to the hilt,
Some biscuits bust and Cameron kilt,
They'll carry all our fondest wishes
And I hope a stock of little fishes.

A canteen manager must be found
For Burnetts knees are not too sound,
The till he's taking home to blighty,
To buy himself a Tartan nightie.

As C.S.M. they will have Baines,
If he keeps afloat there when it rains,
And for a quarter bloke they'll try,
The one & only George Mackay.

The crawls will have to be rehearsed,
In T.O.E.Ts they'll be well versed,
While in Civvy Street, we read the worst,
The horse we backed has not run first.

At 6-15 when they're on P.T.
We'll think of them the wife and me,
And instead of 11 Drill parade,
We'll be mopping back our lemonade.

Our secret weapons will not go,
I mean Louie and Angelo,
For if they holler out Tiecanus,
They'll surly bring the stonk down on us.

Epilogue

Just picture me in Egertons Bar,
A bowler hat and an Africa Star,
A frothy pint and a "braw wee" half,
And Round my neck the Cameron Scarf.

GILLESPIE'S SUCCESS

That lads tried hard the sergeant said,
I can see the way he makes his bed,
A no bad soldier, I have the notion,
To put his name in for promotion.

They wrote his name down in Red Ink,
To make the blokes sit back and think,
Gave him one unpaid & local acting
And endless duties so exacting.

As he sewed the stripe upon his arm,
He tried so hard to keep quite calm,
A carefree smile was on his face,
A blushing flush you too could trace.

He marched from the barracks head erect,
His martial movements quite perfect,
To post a letter home to mother,
To say "I'm Important" like my brother.

The C.O.s words beat in his ears,
"Your foots on the ladder" after 10 years,
And being quite a mathematician,
He knew in 10 more he'd have a higher position.

He faced many dangers & kept so serene,
And many the horrors he'd often seen,
But when Murphy sees him – and stands back aghast,
He'll be like a ship that's been robbed of its mast.

He expected salutes, but received not a one,
What parade in the ranks, just like he'd none.
How could people see him in such a crowd,
Or gaze on that strip, that made him so proud.

We must have a moral to end it all,
To finish this poem of the new Corporal,
If you knew Gillespie as well as we do,
Then before the months out, you ought to have TWO.

*   *   *   *   *

In the North African Desert.

TO ONE WHO IS ABOUT TO DIE
– IT MIGHT HAVE BEEN SOONER

We were the forward section – Murphy, Gardner & Barker were in my gun –pit or trench – The dawn came up and two kids moaned about " wasted time" and home. – The Coy was moving up and we came out – Within a few minutes the 2 little white-armed lads of 18 were dead – As far as I could tell these lads had seen nothing of life, a couple of drunks and a night or two out.

Now let us count our blessings when the time comes that we survived so much longer.

Incidentally when we got to "B" echelon there were parcels from Mummy for both the lads.

GILLESPIE'S DOWNFALL

It was quite early when he rose,
To dress himself in highland clothes,
The Lance Naik of Battalion Guard,
A post he'd tried for extra hard.

He tip-toed past the loudest snorer,
To shave himself with a Minora,
And washed around his dirty knees,
In case the Adjutant he'd displease.

In time his kilt he did adjust,
And from his boots removed the dust,
And twixt the times I mentioned now,
Devoured what Yankees call their chow.

He beezed his badge & bayonet too,
Hitched his hose an inch or two,
And then what seems to you a trifle,
Spent ½ an hour upon his rifle.

The band played "Whiter than the snow",
As down the stairs he had to go,
And looking smart as Annie Laurie,
Took his place upon the lorry.

The venue Adolf Hitler Strasse,
In which to face the Jerry mass,
And let a conquered people see,
The pick of Scotland's Infantry.

All were nervous felt the strain,
The orderly buff was not too plain,
But observing pauses brilliantly,
They did perform most excellently.

Alas it came "Examine Arms",
And sounding like the Fire Alarms,
The Company Orderly's wanted now,
The new Lance Naik is for a row.

"My God" I see a speck of dust,
For this you know – you can get bust,
Bring him up – yes on Report,
The Corporals hopes are down to naught.

The pipes play up he struggles on,
The Lament to Mrs Gillespie's son,
Then to the Guardroom comes dismiss,
Oh heavenly word, oh joyful bliss.

O'er the final scene – we draw the veil,
You can see the corporal looks so pale,
A speck of dust, had spelt his ruin,
Just you watch out, mind what you're doin.

Epilogue

The Lance Naik blessed his stars that,
He hadn't had inspections at,
Medjez, Sousse, or else at *Fet,*
For if he had, he'd be goaled yet,
And never have the dough to get,
That will be his certain bet,
When the only barrel he will know,
Will belong to *McEwan Sons & Co.*
The speck of dust he'll swill away,
And then be happy, young, and gay.

OSTER – REICH

I know I'm wrong when I write all this,
And I've not been swayed by a frauline's kiss,
But there are some things I must express,
About the lands of Rudolf Hess.

To avoid all further explanations,
I suffer not hallucinations,
And in conclusion would make reference,
That for foreign lands I had no preference.

We flew into the Oster-reich,
It was much quicker than a bike,
And must confess we expected trouble,
In smashed up towns like heaps of rubble.

But what we saw were scenes of beauty,
"Boosted" by some blonde haired "cutie",
The craggy Alps in silhouette,
Too far away for climbing yet.

FACTS

(Vide. Daily Express)
June 1945.

It has been ascertained as a result of a full enquiry that the high earnings of the Twelve Liverpool Dockers mentioned in a recent parliamentary question was due in most part to the period mentioned being a holiday, viz Easter.
The highest earning by one man for that week was £42 -12s – 7d and the average was £38 – 7s – 6d. It must be taken into consideration that double time for Good Friday, Saturday, Sunday & Monday brought the total high, and it must be noted that the usual wage drawn by a docker is £7 to £9 a week. The men were engaged in unloading, motor vehicles.

Post War credits £31 – 10s – 0d. !!

At Umberto's Palace near Naples.

BILLETS

Fall out 7 Platoon this is yours,
The one mit Iron & Wooden doors,
It looks as if it's been a beer house,
In which did "Ted" his troubles dowse.

First room on left is One Section,
The Sergeant bawls out this direction,
While up the stair in a Cosy bed,
I'm going to kip in style he said.

True to his word he left us all,
Gellatlys crew will sweep the hall,
While the Brains Trust of Platoon H.Q,
Have got the blinking Street to do.

A figure passes a great attraction,
The young girl speaks we are all action,
I sink I speak a little English,
She says to us – with a deal of relish.

We find her name is Elizabeth,
The prettiest girl since the Mareth,
To attract attention there are many
Who play with baby sister Lennie.

Her mother too has been a smasher,
While Pop does sport a Hitler tasher,
Two boys complete the family roll,
Except for the mare which is in foal.

She presses here & there a shirt,
Or from some pants removes the dirt,
And they've been known to give an egg
Without us giving them a "Meg".

From strength to strength we do go on,
Ellis remains when you are gone,
But one & all we pump the water,
For the Butcher's pretty daughter.

I should have said, as well as beer,
You find the sign, Meat is sold here,
And father has such killing habits,
From cows & calves to little rabbits.

There's one thing does the scene so mar,
You can just sense it from afar,
It oozes forth a nasty smell,
The Latrine position us to tell.

I could go on like Tennyson's River,
About this home of meat & liver,
But suffice it just for me to say,
It'll be a sorry day – when we go away.

*   *   *   *   *

DESCRIPTION

THE ARMY: X X X X

ITALY: Picture an old-type house having had little or no cleaning for years, when all the dust from the grate has settled on the objects in the room.

FRENCH – AFRICANS: Tight, women dressy but living places, par bon, very often cattle in the living rooms.

GREEKS: Procession crazy, definitely Pro-British, Dusty, heat more humid than Africa, dirty Salonika every other shop a Café Cabaret. Patras friendly town. Athens like Rome, Napoli.

CLOSETS: How lucky we are to sit and pander instead of balancing & pirouetting over a tiny grid, or to see paper float away instead of having to see a receptacle full in a toilet box. In many places in Italy they fill a bowl under the stairs, and then sling it through the window.

MILAN: Great Railway all electric. City of Fur Coats.

THE DAY AT THE RACES

(6th Armoured Div. Austria.)

The day dawned fair and all was set,
Thank God the going wasn't wet,
For I when dressed in Sunday best,
Was off my wages to invest.

To tell the truth my destination,
I give to you, no hesitation,
The racecourse out at Eibelhof,
To gamble cash, the Amateur Toff.

Not for me the 1/- wires
Or tips from Pinks or Daily Liars,
I've had it straight from those who know,
The one that will bring in the dough.

I smile the smile of smug content,
For a ¼ hour my schillings lent,
Ere I return to gather in,
Enough to buy a case of gin.

That's just my manner forecasting low,
It doesn't do to boast you know,
But when the race is duly won,
I'll count my schillings by the ton.

I watch the mugs that take a chance,
Lose their cash – on Maggies Romance,
And observe the Aberdonian Race,
Backing the horses, but only for place.

Time flies & soon at 3 – fifteen,
From out the maze of colour green,
Appears Gods Gift to Cameron Men,
God rest its soul – we say – Amen.

Observe your card the name's Delotti,
Just the job it rhymes with Scottie,
The colours White with Tartan Sash,
Its rider the Major with Black Moustache.

He carries out the known routine,
Of walking the Enclosure & being seen,
The saddle goes on – the hour is zero,
Lead out the beast – then ride like a hero.

The field is small we know the reason,
The starts the best we've had this season,
They're in a line, as they take the fence,
It's early yet for thrills to commence.

The Rozzer is backed a cert to win,
His jockey is wearing a confident grin,
But behold Major Burns in the black cap,
As he gives Delotti a wakening tap.

Away she goes like the breath of spring,
All our hearts begin to sing,
There's nothing with her, she runs alone,
All bar Camerons start to groan.

Who put those fences in the way,
To spoil our hopes of wealth today,
We can see they're driving potty.
Our flying filly Miss Delotti.

Just like a dame, she takes the whim,
To throw the jockey, get rid of him,
Stopping quite suddenly, refusing to jump,
Away goes her rider, lands with a bump.

The Grass once green is now a brown,
I grasp the rails, I'm falling down,
The World for me is now a heap,
Oh hang it all! I start to weep.

My Release Group now is No. 3
My Age is nearly Sixty three,
I say Goodbye to my two schilling,
Anyway Racings not so thrilling.

Then in my path stands he who knew,
Whose height is only 5ft two,
He greets me with an alibi,
"I tink I smack him to lullabye".

And then my better soul arose,
Says – adopt, that Independent pose,
And resume your place back in the ranks,
Too much procedure, dealing with Banks.

I've had enough, I'm away back home,
Until in my path, "small man does roam",
Next time out just try Cogalina,
Already my valley is looking much greener.

*Note: History records that the fortnight
after this meeting Cogalina ran, she was
heavily backed, the small man letting
his knowledge spread to a wider sphere.
Cogalina passed the post, but after
about 15 other runners.*

I was like a father figure to the younger lads; many are referred to in the poems: The Last Round Up *and* Under 26s Lament.

THE LAST ROUND-UP

The aged and weary ones go first,
The 24 Group read the worst,
And huddle up in sundry spots,
The utility & the Home Grown Scots,
To find out who was first on earth,
The hour and then the date of birth.

Soon the names on board appear,
The dates and times they disappear,
And trysts and toasts are drunk in plenty,
Some sup one and others twenty,
Very many finish stinking
From excessive Vino drinking.

Some are patted on the back,
Some are beaten up alack,
Of the latter there aren't many,
Better still if there weren't any,
The tears drip down like rain from heaven,
As Camerons leave to report to Bevin.

CAPT. Q. M.

Holy, Holy Holy, Lord God Almighty,
I, the quarter bloke, out from blighty,
What the hell and dam it all,
His swears, and curses us appal. *(One hell but two for him)*

He bellows forth in voice like thunder,
Does he think we're deaf I wonder,
Hey! Here you, in small Balmoral,
He, says its something quite immoral.

He knows it all, until you test-him,
Even then you'll never best-him,
For hasn't he the three bright pips
The power to put you in the "slips".

He claps his hand and Batman Holt,
Dashes up like thunderbolt,
But breathing hard like Mrs Randles,
Blows out alas – the Klipsied candles.

He caught me out, once, in his Jeep,
The things he said made my flesh creep,
And when he said Awa' Be Gone,
Said watch that stripe my only one.

Still I guess somebody loves him,
He is somebody's Cherubim,
Perhaps he is misunderstood,
You don't agree – Who thought you would.

GILLESPIE'S LEAVE

Complete with mop and biscuit tin,
In which to put some water in,
The sergeant Major saw me thus,
And called me over without a fuss.

You're due a leave aren't you Lance Naik,
Seven days at Velden would you like,
It hits me like a Louis Crack,
I nearly have a heart attack.

I murmur out a hearty thanks,
Forget about the Water tanks,
And go to tell my desert friend,
And see what "dust" he has to lend.

Gosh! you're lucky, blokes say to me,
Forget I've none since 43,
In fact to put it in clerical ways
I haven't had one for 1003 days.

Then came the time to pack my kit,
Get my clothes creased up a bit,
And pack away the T M G
No longer any use to me.

I meet the storeman show a grin,
Throw my Derry Bundle In.
Away I go for my F.F.I.,
A prelude to the bye and bye.

I stood there in my birthday suit,
Didn't even wear a boot,
And the M.O. with a curious glance,
Says O.K. – put on your pants.

He knew I'd played the game alright,
Kept all women out of sight,
And never sat upon a seat,
Until I'd seen that all was all-reet.

Soon dressed I walk into the hall,
Where on my ears did chance to fall,
The news that two men would not go,
Until the Orderly Room said so.

Of course they gave the men a name,
All the boys said what a shame
The names omitted were to be,
Pte. Boyd and Lance Naik Me.

I praised the Army system well,
And wished the Orderly Room in hell,
Gave all the up & ups 3 cheers,
And burst into a flood of tears.

Now in the barracks I sit & think,
Of how the First & Eighth did link,
How I missed the leave at Philippeville,
Which eludes me now & ever will.

PHIL BROWN *(one scouse)*

Knew his brother,
Saw his mother,
Same Town
Name Brown
A definite no-user.

Joined the Scottish,
Not standoffish,
Company X
Sun Specs.

Has Blue Eyes,
Tells no lies,
Stripes One,
Ones gone.

Drives a Truck,
Likes a Duck,
Driver Mech,
Sorts a wreck.

His name's Phil,
Assets Nil,
Dormant Brains,
Varicose Veins.

A Massive body,
Never shoddy,
Curly Hair,
Doesn't swear.

A 'D' Day Dodger,
A Cairo Lodger,
Abroad late,
Had to wait.

Knows his mines,
Likes his wines,
Dead Keen,
A Has-been.

Has sweaty feet,
Sings a treat,
Always late,
What a mate,

Took a wife,
Ruined her life,
Some Father,
All Blather.

I'll run him down,
This geezer Brown,
Always Tapping,
Else napping
<u>There you have Phil Brown</u>.

FAREWELL

Phil Brown is in 23 Group, I have just left him, he has had a "Grand send
off", grand singing, and not the least a few poems. Gordon Lennie excuses
himself for being absent through duty, but says: "I just had to see you, I
always liked you. Cpl. Tom Dawson. M.M. grabbed him by the hand and
said "You're a great lad Brown, I wish there were thousands like you, I'm
only sorry I've not had the pleasure of soldiering through with you. Good
Luck".
    He stood there with his cap under his arm, a medal for every
campaign across his chest, and a bottle of whisky unopened within his
reach. The time was 10 pm. And he had been offering his bottle to
members of his Platoon since the Canteen opening hour. A small man held
the door fast, another taller man a little worse for drink, pushed the
bemedalled warrior, and a chain of men circled the other exit, one or two
N.C.O's moved out, I heard the "bark" of a tree outside and went to
investigate. Sergeant Burns was going home – it's strange the different
ways people have of expressing their likes and dislikes.
    I scarcely took a drink, this parting night, I was the only duty man
leaving, but boxing carefully I kept sipping the same pint. Nearly all the
"old gang" were in Rome or else away home, the last I remember was a
quartette of Careless, Pinches, Ashwood and Montague singing "Lead
Kindly Light" and "We'll meet again". Baxter saw me to my bed, a
ceremonial he insisted on, in two years he will follow.

A HERO

I dare not write this while I am with the company, for should the person referred to see or read it, my life would be in danger.
This is my definition of a hero, a universally popular figure in the Camerons, and I am proud to say an ex Liverpool Scottish.

He will come home without VC
Or medals for valour of any degree,
The neighbours will note Italian Star,
Some will remark he ain't been far.

His name was in orders once I believe,
Some note had been taken of what he did achieve,
Mentioned in despatches so we read
Encore their "Savoy" – then went to bed.

He never went brawling or waking the dead,
Or booked our names for being in bed,
As a Regimental Naik, he was a dead loss,
To cause him to panic – was just Imposs.

Ask for the one who all men would be,
Happy to be with on Hill 63,
Or ask which man in coolness excels,
The answer near always will be Bob Wells.

He scarcely if ever turned a hair,
When Jerry dirt was in the air,
Although his guts like yours and mine
Must have been quaking in the line.

He came through battle a little tired
It took some months ere knowledge I acquired,
That our Ruby Robert wasn't well,
In fact his nervous system was all to hell.

He left us in Greece went into dock,
Much regretted by each & every man jock,
And after a considerable lapse of time,
Returned to our Unit, not in his prime.

This is where the manhood shows,
His inner feelings no one here knows,
He's san fairy ann – Alakeefic all right,
No moaning, no groaning, he's always so bright.

That's courage, by God, its well above par,
Not killing Germans, but greater by far,
It's harder to fight that kind of fear,
Than the one when the Jerries somewhere are near.

I'm away home now, Bob, but I'd just like to say,
That's what seven Platoon asked me today,
To express their thanks, in few words of Rhyme,
For your Courage & Comradeship all of the time.

The Liverpool Scottish Regiment at camp prior to World War II.
Courtesy of 'The Liverpool Scottish Museum Trust'.

ARNOLD'S CARDBOARD BOX

In Pantomime Aladdin had a magic lamp,
In Politics, old Neville had a plain old gamp,
In Movies "Leggy" Grable had such lovely frocks,
In Reality our Arnold had his cardboard Box.

As he wanders forth from Railway Train,
Swearing never to stand again,
Shabby, Shoddy and travel stained,
Looking for Freedom which he'd now gained.

I suppose you wonder what was found,
Inside the box so square, not round,
Keep it dark in case he's robbed,
His Civvy Clothes – He's been demobbed.

He clutched it to his panting heart,
In case from it he'd have to part,
And looking like a hunted rabbit,
Wiped his nose on sleeve from habit.

He stops on platform, and looks not for Bents,
But for the signboard – "In Here for the Gents".
It's excitement & journeys that's made him so free,
But he's no time to lose, between thee and me.

Cardboard boxes are O.K., walking down streets,
Or for nice milky chocolates or fancy sweets,
But Arnold felt humbled as he struggled for penny,
He found himself wishing that he hadn't any.

The Green turned to yellow as penny did click,
And Arnold was sweating – being so quick,
The end was so tragic – a trifle grim,
Yes room for the box, but no room for him.

Although on Army manoeuvres he'd won renown,
Arnold had "had it" before they were down,
No scribbled message needed to tell,
Trust your own judgement – follow the smell.

It's happened at weddings, also on runs,
Its often be caused by mortars & guns,
So don't stare at Arnold whenever he's round
And leave no cardboard boxes there to be found.

He gets so annoyed, when he thinks on the day,
It's so "Infra Dig" to finish that way,
Thank goodness he hadn't had on his white socks,
Or been seen by his mates of the Liverpool Jocks.

13 January 1946.

PASSING THOUGHTS

How the end of the War caused little or no excitement. – How the fact that the ship you are on may be torpedoed, is an accepted fact, and you are not afraid. – The value of Drinking Water – The Church Parade waiting for the commencement of the Service – The great opportunity missed by the Church, a golden opportunity to save the world – The lack of "Woodbine Willies".

The "shake" you get when your L.E.A.P. is due, headaches, quivering fingers, etc. The power of the press how they change their views, and incidentally your own. The fleeting glimpses you have in your minds eye of the places you're in.

The heap of tripe you see in Newspapers at home. The British party had a grand welcome off the Bulgarians. — So did "A" Coy.

Can we who are safe ever recapture again all the misery vividly enough – to describe it for other – "would be after it's all over " – killers. God only knows what Arnhem was like, thank Christ I wasn't there, somebody failed to give the boys an even money chance. They that live get "the glory" (the inward satisfaction)), but after a year or two they will be apologising for having dodged it out there, and not roughed it at Napiers, Rootes etc., – Why High ranking German Officers were allowed to roam around without escort – when one was taken back the reply was – "you can't touch him" he has given his word, he is on parole. Meanwhile the call ups herded in the open behind the wire.

VICTORY OVER GERMANY

All through my days in the Army my wish had been for this day, "The Millennium" of every soldier. Now it was here – and very little excitement did it cause, a decided apathy existing. This was no doubt due to our geographical position – viz: near the Bulgarian border, "bivvying out" with nothing but great craggy peaks, and gorse lands. The nearest village about 16 Kilo's (about 10 miles), was the only place were existed the possibility of "letting off steam". That it was essential to get cracking, was recognized by both Phil Brown and myself. We both drank heavily, nothing else for it, and yet all the while when our joy should have been terrific, one could only think of the boys that had "passed away". Finally quantity told, and we both had black-outs, and had to walk back at 5am, we were called over the coals, but not punished this time.
LIAR!

V.J. DAY

After Six years the day for which we civilians had lived and prayed each night came, our War was over, but the drafts of men were still leaving the Battalion for home and then Burma, when the end came so suddenly, many rumours had been floating about, but it seemed impossible. Now whether it was the end, or not we were brought to our feet. Drill parade, shouting the time out, we were the winners, liberators, crusaders, call us as you like, fighting men, treated mostly as children, bad children. We were it was announced to have a holiday of two days in the near future. It came I was a guard the first day, and dismounted the second day at 9.30 am. *Oh blessed day.*

28 DAYS LEAVE HOME TO ANGLETERRE

We started out at 3.am. on the Morning (Sunday), and travelled in a rather congested fashion to Padua some 50 to 60 miles away. The awakening had been a rude one, two or three taps and a kick, and with the temperature at freezing point, (Khaki Drill was a little out of fashion) tempers of "canned" personnel were a little 'testy'.

The stretcher cases being duly placed aboard, we sallied forth to the outside world, bound for all those near and dear to us. We had covered 110 miles by 9-30 am, just marking time, for we again passed our starting point at this hour. The first day saw us in Brescia, Trento, by-passing Milan, and by night we had raced through the Brenner Pass, where our driver hit the first bridge out, we were white, scared for a few minutes, but we were towed in last, but not least.

It was raining, our billet was a stable with a colander roof, I slept well, imagining myself a large Aspidistra plant, and Cecil Lewis was watering me.

We rose early, and found our bath prepared, a pool in the doorway. Rain still battered down and a lorry that leaked similar to our billet came into the possession of we three (Cpls. Allcott, Phillips and self). It was smashing to be able to breathe freely and after ½ days travel we had got into fine weather, and we placed our beds down. This was the forerunner of many pleasant days, as travelling in the rear of a vehicle, it can be quite cold, even when the outside world is enjoying a reasonably warm day. Austria looked as pretty as ever, the grass and leaves look the brightest green you have ever seen, and the chalets, looked so clean and well-made in comparison with Italian and Francaise contraptions. We passed through Germany, and believe me when I say that scarcely a house is standing, in Mainz for instance everything had "had it" and the city is a very large one, even the Cathedral had partly caved in.

Then we arrived at the Luxemburg border, spoke to a dame, then on to the French frontier, and the gay French. As usual they took on the air of being happy as a "dead bird", in fact these "jolly folk" seem to have had an extra long break from their Gay and youthful zest, the order to resume laughing should be given. We arrived at Calais, welcome as Liberators, silk stockings £2- 5s – 0d, small Vermouth 3/4d per glass. After a night's sleep we embarked at 8 am, and reached HOME in a little over the hour. With very little palaver we passed through the Customs, on to our train, for a two hours run to Victoria Station London; after which we made our own way to The Casa, Maison, Haus, which was and had been a prime thought in our head ever since we left home. The first civilian apart from the Railway Station Master was a Woman. You see, there were no bands, or cheering crowds, this was something that was happening at Folkestone, twice or thrice a day, but this lady struck all the chords of thanks and welcome in one minute. Phillips and I felt good, so much that even though we were standing in the corridor we felt on top of the world, and being so hardy, we ignored the Railway precautions and put our heads through the window frame. The old lady was in black, and after waving her handkerchief she wiped (or appeared to) her eyes, Phillips had a tear he couldn't stop, and I likewise. The other outstanding features were the signs on walls of gable ends, God Bless you All – Thanks for what you've done, and supplementing all this in back gardens, people (who no doubt had relatives similarly as unfortunate as ourselves) waved across to us. It was enough, we are a very sentimental race.

We reached London, and then were transferred to Euston by Bus for the final Run-In. The fleeting glimpse of London showed that the United Nations were well dug in, (I say this literally) and I suppose that I must mention we saw one English Girl with a soldier of our own country, who she was, will remain to me a mystery, she may have of course – been the boys sister. The streets we passed through of course were not the "homely type" we all think about, only the ones we make for on recreation bent, unless like Cecil Lewis we revolve in the upper circle.

The train I took to Liverpool stopped at every station almost, and I felt tired as I listened to a Stoke on Trent woman giving her husband a dog's life because the train was 8 minutes late. He "kept the head", helped her adjust her varicose veins and assisted her in the removal of 4 portmanteaus, upon their arrival.

I arrived at Lime Street, five minutes to closing time, and to my horror "the bars were up", (shades of the desert). Excitement was intense, Salute the soldier Week was finishing, everyone was "stinking", probably of their friends. After a considerable lapse of time waiting for Car, Bus or Taxi, a Yankee officer came over and said its all lip worship, this flag wagging, and I agreed with him. Eventually a "girl" conductor allowed me aboard, an already crowded tram.

I reached May's mothers home at 11-15, the re-union is not for publication, and there we found Jean sleeping, so did not wake her. She woke early next morning, and came to the bedroom and then I noted the change in her. She was a splendid conversationalist, and we got on very well, all my leave. She had a habit of backing out of the room holding with her left hand, the splits in the back of her pyjamas.

May had not altered any, though, along with her mother, had been taking a little interest in politics. The leave was marvellous, every second was one round of enjoyment, and not forgettable. The last few days were tragic, all the wind was out of my sails, I got an extension, by courtesy of the weather man (Gales in the channel) of 4 days. Pardon me for saying got – received is the word. Still it had to come 1pm 1st Nov., to the last strains of Workers Playtime or Works Wonders, with the girls voices predominating they sang "Coming Home my darling". I plucked up courage, and went to say Cheerio to Jean, she hugged me and started to cry out "I don't want you to go", and "I don't want daddy to go". I continued to look from the window at the trams and buses below, wheeled about kissed Ma, and grabbed my kit-bag. At the door May was waiting, we embraced, no words, then I was through the door, into the street. I must say I looked and they were all waving after me, then unlike the quiet silent man in deep contemplation, I subjected Warfare, Armies, etc., to condemnation. The journey back was horrible jammed in trains, no sleep, little food, and what there is must be queued for, hours on end. There are no saving clauses – it's deadly – and I thank God that I will not be going through that Home-leaving ordeal in another 3 years hence. Within a couple of days I was on Regimental Quarter Guard, followed by Battalion Orderly Corporal, and a Medical Inspection pending my Release in Group. 24.

RETURN TO HAPPINESS ON A ONE WAY TICKET

Date leaving Unit ...18 Dec. 1945.
Date of Arrival in Blighty ...30 Dec. 1945.

Instruction – Upon arrival in England the bearer of Release Book will be fully qualified to stand in a queue of any length or depth. He will have suffered in these days every inconvenience that can be placed in his way, he will neither sit in a reasonable space, or receive in his mess tin or plate (stolen) the fruits of the field (or factory manufacture) unless it has been murdered or destroyed of food value, and the portion allotted to him will consist of the ration given to one sparrow or dormouse. In event of any person presuming to have upon his face anything in the nature of a smile, care will be taken to see that unnecessary parades and prolonged stays in transit will remove same. If the bearer of the aforesaid Release Book will ponder awhile, he will have recollections of seeing Release Men sitting in big easy chairs, a pint of beer at their elbow, and a few of their companions playing Billiards and Snooker, a door leading off says "Civvy Street". This was the theory the "practice" was not in alignment. It is a very poor answer to this statement of facts, "that any man coming out of the Army will not mind going through this to get out". A triumph of Dis-organisation, when things get moving, they will no doubt improve, when 66 Group come out. At present everything is "Laid on", particularly the Draft. Still – Praise the Lord I finish this book as John Gillespie, Esquire complete with one Grey suit, one Raincoat, one Shirt and 2 collars, One trilby hat, one pair Shoes, and two pairs of socks all Civilian Mark One pattern, and 93 days leave in lieu of services rendered, and articles "vendered".

God Save the King.

To The Clanging of Bells, and marching music of the Bands of many Regiments.

FINIS

Just in case the contents make you imagine that to the Victor go the spoils, as briefly as possible I append these true facts :-

From the Solicitor: "Dear Mr Gillespie – In spite of the many requests that he vacate your furnished house 2, Ebenezer Rd., your Mr Davies (tenant) still remains on fixed lines – I am therefore taking final action".
W. J. McMillan.

From the Firm – Extract:

"This is a commission I could well have done without, it is not easy to tell an old & faithful servant his services are no longer required. We trust that you will soon be successful in finding a good post".

Newspaper cutting: We join "Eight Toolmakers" in expressing indignation that "ex servicemen should receive preferential treatment as regards housing. The Government decided that we should be soldiers in "Civvies". (This inside six months of the War finishing).

CONCLUSION

You will be as daft as your Dad or Uncles and "have a go".

AFTER THE WAR

*My wife and I with one of our racehorses in 1966. During this period I was
Export Manager at Hurcott Paper Mills in the Worcestershire countryside.
I wrote the poem 'The Touch' around this time.*

THE TOUCH

(Written twenty years after the war)

I vainly sought to find the touch whereby I could impart
Upon a canvas white and bare, all that was in my heart.
Which on fulfilment would reflect, to me a lifetime's pleasure
A reality on which to gaze, appraise and oftimes treasure.

Without success I then took pen, and proceeded to set down
Line by line of poetry using verb and noun,
Chosen words all set in rhyme, whose object was for me,
To relive again those blessed days, the days that used to be.

My restless spirit urges me to try to write a play,
Recording varied incidents experienced day by day.
Sad to relate, it isn't great, this achievement when completed
Bereft of touch, and without flair, it leaves me still defeated.

In music then I seek solace, attempt and write a score
An opera and a minuet which critics do encore,
But very plain for all to see, no master's hand is here,
Equivalents are daily writ, on this great worldly sphere.

My passion wilts just for a while, where must I turn to next?
I read the lines of greater men, in psalms I seek a text
Hurried changes into flurried, my vision is impaired,
Such is the haste within my breast, I cannot see a word.

"Call it a day", most folk say, why not cry a halt?
Admit to failure, no, not I, or any worth his salt.
Rest from work that will I do, my pens I'll lay aside
And for a while I'll anger then, my tarnished battered pride.

Within the workshop of my brain, the search continues on,
Whilst outwardly I seem quite calm and all ambition gone,
I climb the hills and craggy tops; I wander in the field,
The fruits of these diversities at last begin to yield.

Refreshed by slumbers quite serene, the sights I see are new,
Land that once was derelict has now become a view
Conveying to the dormant mind, this is no time to rest,
Indeed the most appropriate whereto resume my quest.

"There's none so blind as cannot see" all people do agree,
Now full well I realise how this applies to me.
For that I've searched so urgently is now within my clutch,
A vivid pattern in my brain, that will supply "The Touch".

I set my canvas and start to paint, more eager than before,
And from my brush to my great joy, the touch begins to pour.
I print the title bold and clear "The Garden of my Life"
And dedicate my masterpiece to my darling wife.

In the corner the two gnarled trees stand for Mum and me,
While the nearby bushes sprouting green, are the family.
Here and there the wisps of straw, which from outside have blown,
Stand for ills and trials that in our life we've known.

The path well worn but deadly straight, conveys a way of life,
Whilst the damaged hedge portrays for me the pangs of war and strife.
The weeds, and they are countless, flourish in the sun,
To signify the blunders and the tasks I left undone.

A beauty parlour of flower beds, with buds of every hue,
Red, pink, violet, heliotrope and blue,
Roses, tulips, daffodils, with each other vie,
In this blaze of glory, to try to catch the eye.

Birds that fly up to the tree, or peck upon the lawn
Illustrate full well to me, our work from dusk to dawn.
The lazy twisting little stream, with water crystal clear,
Personifies an endless time, the drift from year to year.

The final joy is painting in, a golden yellow sun,
Surveying there omnipotent, the work he had begun.
You can see from largest tree down to the smallest sod,
A response gesture reaching out, "Accept our thanks oh God".

AN ODE TO AN 86 YEAR-OLD FOOL

(Poem penned fifty years after the war)

If only I had listened when I was at school,
I wouldn't wear this label, branding me a fool.
I could run a government – tell folk what to do,
Most minutes would be taken up with boasting what I knew.

If only I had listened I could be the one to teach,
I could take a congregation and to them I could preach.
I could fix them up for heaven and see that some got wed.
No people would be starving – second helpings would be fed.

Problems I would iron out, larger gatherings I'd address,
Every project I began would be a great success,
The children they would wave to me – some indeed would bow,
Which is alas so different from what is happing now.

If all my crusts I'd eaten, my hair would hang in curls
Instead upon my baldy pate, flies skate and try out whirls.
If only I had listened I'd be a wizard in a quiz.
Instead I'm being beaten by James and baby Liz.

Sometimes as encouragement they pat me on the head
But very often they suggest its time I was in bed.
So sad I didn't listen, or do extra work at home
But allowed both my thoughts and feet often far to roam.

If I'd listened to Miss Stopperton the piano I could play,
Sad to say I didn't, and from practice ran away.
So now I pay the penalty of perpetual shame –
Couldn't even do his sums – couldn't write his name!

AN ODE TO A WALKING STICK

*(Dedicated to Queen Elizabeth the Queen Mother
upon her leaving hospital 23rd February 1998)*

Fall in love with a walking stick
    Seems a silly thing to do.
But it isn't when you come to think
    Of all it does for you.
It flicks aside the curtains
    That are above your head.
Then stays with you throughout the day,
    Once you get out of bed.

Your dress it lifts
    From highest hook
Pulls in for you
    The oft dropped book
It taps the floor -
    'Folks know' you're alive!
In the land that I live in,
    A cup of tea will arrive.

As I clutch the stick firmly,
    I mind the day.
When I was out shopping,
    With my darling May.
We saw the stick looking
    So supreme on the rack.
"You like it? – I'll buy it"
    Says May then, to Jack.

Think of the time when
    That hefty young thug,
Glared and demanded
    Or else he would mug.
"Pay or you've had it"
    He'd leave you for dead
He's dispatched by the stick
    With one blow to the head.

When time comes for bed,
   Perhaps, twelve o'clock.
The stick always helps
   In removing your sock.
Press the stick on the toe-end,
   Then slide out the feet.
Just to ease all that bending,
   Is a real 'special' treat.

Then you climb into bed.
   Snuggle in, twixt the sheets.
Having first put the lid
   On your new tin of sweets,
You declare it's "lights out"
   When the switch you do flick.
Who does that? You've guessed it,
   Of course it's – the stick!

It doesn't boast.
   It doesn't scream.
Won't brag about hooking,
   A kid from a stream.
Come let me polish you,
   Make you look smart.
For when I say thank you,
   It's straight from the heart.

_____

GLOSSARY

Alack ....sadly
Alakeefic ....Army slang "couldn't care less"
'B' Echelon..................Base for soldiers
Bents ....Brewery
Bernard Law...............'Monty' Field Marshal Montgomery
Bevin............................U.K. War Minister.
Bivvying......................bivouac in tents
Buckshee.....................slang – something extra of little worth
C.S.M. ....Company Sergeant Major
Don. Rs........................Despatch Riders
F.F.I..............................free from infection
Havildar......................name for a sergeant in the British Indian Army
Imshee.........................Arab expression 'clear off'
Klipsied.......................pinched or stolen.
Korda...........................Film Producer
L.E.A.P. ....soldier's leave
Mareth.........................French built defensive line in Tunisia
Meg..............................halfpenny
Minora.........................shaving razor
Mit ....between
M.O..............................Medical Officer
M.T...............................Motor Transport
Neville's gamp...........Chamberlain's umbrella
Nix ....nothing
Pal Blades ....brand of razor blades
P.K...............................brand of spearmint
Naik.............................Corporal in the British Indian Army
Rank ....Film Producer
R/E. Jobs....................Regimentally Employed
Tee-chai ....Ghurkha name for tea.
Tiecanus ....Greek "Tikanis Kala" 'how are you'.
T.M.G...........................Thomson Machine Gun
T.O.E.Ts ....Test of Elementary Training in weapons
Velden ....a town in Austria
Von Armin ....German General in the Great War